Walking A Country Road

Audrey E. Simonson

To order additional copies of this book, contact:
Xlibris
844-714-8691
www.Xlibris.com
Orders@Xlibris.com

ISBN: Softcover   978-1-6641-3261-0
        Hardcover   978-1-6641-3262-7
        EBook   978-1-6641-3260-3

Print information available on the last page

Rev. date: 11/13/2020

Special thanks – Candace and Chris
Photos by Audrey E. Simonson
Cover Photo American Images, Marshfield, WI

To
Marge and Polly
who walked that same country road

Author's Note

    I started writing about the things I saw and heard while walking our country road. The oat field was first, then the birds trying to drive me away from their territory. Most were written in the 1990s and early 2000's. Later, I thought about all the other roads in my life as I sorted my mother's photos. Those essays have been written in the past year, 2020.

    This book is not arranged chronologically. After the introduction of the places I've lived, the essays are arranged from late winter through summer to autumn – autumn in Iowa and the autumn of my life.

    It has been a good life and God has blessed me with great family and friends. My hope is that you will look at nature and life about you and thank God for all He has created.

Contents

Evolution of a Country Road

In the fall of 1942, my family moved to a farm on the west edge of Woodside Township, Ottertail County, Minnesota. I was 3 ½ years old and my brother was barely two.

Our township, or at least our farm and some land to the west, was made up of a series of sandhills, bogs and sloughs. Most of the boggy ground was put into pasture for the dairy cows that sustained every farm in our neighborhood. The sloughs sometimes had enough open water in spring for ducks to swim and my brother and me to sail toy boats.

Somewhere, about a mile and a half west of our farm, the road took a dip in the landscape and disappeared into the sloughs. As I remember, it was not much wider than a car width with willows and cattails on both sides. After a rainy spring, we drove through water to the next hilly spot and then to the highway. How long was that watery stretch? Maybe thirty yards, but it was a LONG way across when I was little.

By the time I was ten the road had been graded to a respectable height and width so there were no more scary adventures dealing with water sloshing the bottom of the car. The kids of today have other scary things to deal with. I'll take water, anytime.

Country School House # 275, Woodside Township, Ottertail
County, Minnesota 1945-1951 on "that road"

The Farm on the 1940's Road

We got electricity when I was about 8 years old. Dad had the house insulated at the same time. More than once my mother commented on what a good house we had compared with those on the neighboring farms.

We never had a telephone, never had a bathroom, had running water only when we pumped the handle of a small pump hooked to a 2-inch pipe pounded into the ground. The sloughs in that part of the county made the water table high enough for a simple pipe. We never had the water tested for chemicals; never had a water heater except the tea kettle on the stove. The pump was in the house, so at least that was an advantage over some of our neighbors!

Not having a telephone was not so much a handicap. If we needed to call anyone there was a telephone 3 miles to the east and 3 miles to the west. When we needed to talk with a neighbor, Dad or Mom drove the pickup, car or tractor to the neighbor's house. In thinking back on this, it was more civilized than an impersonal telephone, especially when party lines made your business - everyone's business.

The Farm in Woodside Township, Ottertail County, Minnesota c. 1955

The Road Into Town - Part 1

The road I live on – 410th Street in Powhatan Township of northeast Pocahontas County, Iowa, is not paved. The paved road, a mile south of our farm, leads another mile west to the little town of Plover, Iowa. Named by railroad executives in the 1800's, Plover is one of three towns along this railroad line named for birds. Mallard and Curlew are the other two. The mallard is a duck. Curlews and plovers are shorebirds with long legs and distinctive vocal calls.

When I moved to Pocahontas County in 1970, Plover had well over 100 citizens. It had a grocery store, beauty shop, gas station, lumber store, one church, a town library, an elementary school, city park, an electrician, an automotive repairman, a cycle shop, a well-drilling company, a building contractor and a grain elevator that held whatever grain the local farmers were able to sell after feeding their cattle and hogs.

As I write this fifty years later, no one lives on that section of land on the north side of the highway east of Plover, where we lived in the '70's. The town has fewer than 50 residents; the elevator and post office are the only remaining businesses. The church was closed last year. The library is open three days a week and offers town and rural residents varied programs throughout the year.

The Town of Plover, Iowa - Sunrise, 2020

The Road Into Town, Part 2

In much of Iowa, the land is divided into square miles by gravel and limestone roads and some paved roads. The prairie allows such regular division. One square mile is divided into quarter sections of 160 acres, which can be divided in half to form two eighty acre sections. Most farms in 1970 were the size of a quarter section. The first farm we lived on in 1970 that we call "the old place" was located on the north side of that paved road leading to Plover – a short three-quarters of a mile walk to town.

That farm was the southeast quarter of the section. Wayne and Helen lived on the southwest quarter. The northwest quarter was divided into two 1/8th sections and were owned and farmed by two different landlords. The northeast section had a house and barn where Jack and Pearl lived. Three families lived in that one section of Iowa farmland.

The square mile where we now live is divided into four sections, farmed by four different families. This square mile has two families – Dave and Wendy on the north edge and Roger and me on the south edge. Since the house and other buildings are relatively new, our expectations are that younger people will live here on this road after we have moved on. I hope they enjoy walking a country road as much as I have.

The Farm East of Plover - 1982

The Old Place

I stop at the "old place" where we lived for twelve years. I sit in the car for a bit, remembering summers spent in this house. The daughter and son born while we lived here are now older than I was when I moved here.

One thing I've missed about the luxury of living on a paved road is that we could open the windows so summer breezes (even refreshing winter breezes) could flow through the house. Only once did we suffer a big dust storm common in the prairie states. I hurriedly closed windows, but it did little good. By the mid-1970's most of the local farmers began conserving the soil by using minimum tillage instead of mold-board plowing. Dust storms ceased to be a problem.

This farm is where we raised hogs the years we lived here and had cows and calves in the winter for forty years. The cattle were on pasture during the summer but in the late fall, winter and early spring they had the surrounding fields to browse for corn or soybeans that may have been left on the ground at harvest.

I drive away thinking of more memories that need to be put into print. Years pass quickly, don't they?

The House on the Highway 1970-1982

The Grove

We built a new house on the southwest quarter in Section 2, Powhatan Township, Pocahontas County, Iowa, starting in 1978 and moved into it in 1982. It took that long because WE built it!! My husband was farming 400 acres by himself, so time was scarce. We had built three metal machine sheds in those first eight years of marriage, so we knew how to work together.

We hired a contractor to dig and build the basement walls and floor, an electrician to do his job and plumbers to get all the pipes in the right places. A shop in town built the cabinetry.

The rest of the building was done by my husband, with the rest of us "holding the end of the board". It has amazed us how much our sons learned about carpentry just by being a helper. Finishing the oak woodwork and painting walls was my job. We were in our early 40's and had the energy to do such a project.

The summer after we moved in, a windbreak was planted on the west and north sides of a couple acres of pasture surrounding the house. Watering the trees every other day for the first two summers was a job our pre-teens hated. Now, their children can explore the "forest".

By the time I started walking the road past our house and the grove, it had grown to substantial size and held more than a few species of birds, rabbits, and often, more than a few deer. They provide entertainment for the miniature horse now occupying the pasture.

Evergreens on the North Side

A Gathering Place

Technically, the weeping birch is not beside the country road but is behind our house. It gives a good balance to the roof line when seen from the road.

The birch was bare this year – bare of leaves, but rarely bare of birds. It took at least a month after the other trees were leafed out before we realized that something was wrong. We decided to let the tree stand because of the beauty of its form.

But what made the tree give up? In travelling this summer, we saw many bare birches. Did disease kill all of them? Was it an ice storm, coming at the worst possible moment in the budding process? The birch was especially beautiful this spring, covered with ice. I will never see ice the same way again.

What leaves usually hid was out in the open this year. Close to the feeders and the bird bath, what better tree could be found? Birds – sometimes dozens at a time – used the tree as a gathering place. They carried on meetings and made challenges. More than a few courtships took place among the branches. Occasionally, more than one species rested there at the same time – robins, goldfinches, sparrows, blackbirds and an occasional grackle. What a lesson in community!

The Willow Tree

Kitty in a Pussy Willow

Sammy was born in our machine shed and lived outdoors at our house for more than a year. He was not quite one year old when I saw him at the top of the pussy willow, determined to get those sparrows! I don't know what he weighed, but it must have been about three pounds.

Willow has been used for centuries to weave sturdy baskets, chair seats and countless other things for mankind to use. I never appreciated the strength of willow until Sammy climbed out on those small branches.

He is a character and kept us entertained while he lived with us. But an old friend needed companionship. She gave me a big hug when I showed her the photo of a cat who needed to be safe in a house.

Soon after he moved there, he disappeared and when the search led her outside, his new mother discovered him in a tree. When called, he scrambled down and leaped into her arms...nearly knocking the lady off her feet. Most endearing to her was when she fell on the floor he came and sat on her lap while she telephoned for help. He used to sit on my lap - the reason I gave him to a lonely friend.

He belongs to a new lady now. She spends winters in Florida while Sammy spends them in a house in Ames, Iowa, with college students.

One winter found him on a road trip to Washington, D.C. That is another story!!

Sammy and the Sparrows

Anticipation

It is only mid-March, yet the grove is full of happy, anticipatory, migratory birds. All kinds of birds! How I wish I'd had a tape recorder on my walk this morning. I try to identify the songs and only a few stand out from the rest.

I hear red-winged blackbirds – their trill is familiar since childhood when my home was surrounded with sloughs, cattails, and those easily-identified red-wings. They seem like old friends.

An occasional crow calls from some of the larger trees across the road from our grove. They've been around all winter and may wonder what all the commotion is about. Later this summer, smaller birds will give chase to those crows, hoping to keep them from robbing their nests.

The robin's song is familiar, too. This time of year their song is not as varied as later in the summer when they have fledglings to educate. Usually the first birds to arrive in the spring, these robins are relative late comers. Are they wondering what is going on with the crowded trees? Do they worry about fighting for the early worm?

The Too-Early Robin

The Bachelor

I first saw him on the front steps in late March. The next time, he was strolling through the back yard, the greens and golds of his neck reflecting in the late afternoon sun. Later, he was in the horse pasture behind the house and, once, he crossed the road ahead of me as I was out for my morning walk.

One spring day, my cat sat in the porch window, crouching, tail switching wildly as a really big bird was in her sight! My movement by the window sent him walking quickly away.

When outside, or when a window was open, I could hear him crowing. There is nothing quite like the sound of a rooster pheasant's crow when he is lonely. I wondered if there was a hen out there who would answer.

One day, while walking a mile south of the house, a hen pheasant crossed the road. "Hey, Bachelor", I called. "Here she is!" But I needn't have worried.

Several days later, two hens walked through the back yard toward the grove. Looking out the west window to check their progress, I started to laugh. The Bachelor emerged from the shadows and followed them. I should have known that a good-looking bachelor can get TWO good-looking chicks!!

Pheasant on the Front Step

Mallards

The spring had been too wet. Crops were not yet planted and water from the fields drained into road ditches where wildlife should have been building nests.

Driving, rather than walking this time, I turned the corner toward our house and started past the ditch with water 6 or more inches deep and extending the length of a football field. There, swimming in the water, were a dozen or more mallards. If I had been walking, the birds would have flown away before I got close. Vehicles were so common, they just kept on swimming.

Getting my camera from the house, I drove back past the birds and turned around at the corner, driving slowly toward the mallards.

They didn't notice the van until I stopped. Before they flew away I got a video of a dozen of them swimming or walking down the sides of the ditch to the water.

Some of the fun of this country road trip was sending the video to my grandsons so they could count the number of mallards.

Sometimes driving a country road is nearly as satisfying as walking!

Ducks in the Ditch

The Oat Field

The first thing I noticed as I drove past the field was the downed oats. Barely green and turning to gold, the grain heads were so heavy the tiny stems could not support them. They were no match for the heavy rain and strong wind the previous night.

Walking the road, I saw how closely planted were the seeds. The Bible verse about "whatsoever a man soweth, so also shall he reap" came to mind. I've seen oat fields planted sparsely and harvested the same. But this field would yield a good harvest.

I paused in my walk. The grain stems were not twisted as they went down, but all laid in the same direction. Knowing rain and wind were probably responsible for the flattened areas seemed such an ordinary explanation and so boring.

In my imagination, a red-winged blackbird lands on a few oat heads. Clutching the oats with his feet and trying to reach down to eat some of the grain puts him off-balance. Wings flapping wildly, he feels the stems bend and go over toward the ground. It is time to fly away from this spot! Circling the field, he sees waves of grain falling, like dominoes, until large areas are flat.

That sounds like a better explanation of downed grain. Ah, the power of the individual!!

Oats Blown Down

Wind In The Night

I thought it was hard rain. Swinging out of bed, I noticed it was a little past one a.m. My husband answered my question, "Rain?" with "Wind!" With an outside light, we could see the rain going sideways from winds of sixty to eighty miles per hour.

The sight of the flattened sweet corn in the morning light was bad enough, but the hundreds of acres of corn tipped and sometimes twisted made us wonder if there had been some devil at work in the night. One field might be standing just as it was the day before, while the field across the fence line would have half of its stalks tipped, some ripped out by the root.

My husband's plan to have good-looking crops in August when visitors arrive from California was blown, too. Maybe this was a truer picture of what farming is all about. We fertilize, cultivate and harvest. But, ultimately, we farm at the mercy of the natural forces on this earth.

Our California guest asked if we irrigate our crops. We said, "No." She asked, "You mean you have to depend on God?" and I heard my son quietly say, "He usually takes care of it."

Flattened Cornfield

Stars in a Bean Field

My favorite time to walk my country road is dusk, when the sun has gone down and the evening breeze is just strong enough to keep mosquitoes at bay. Tonight, the soybean field east of the house was ablaze with hundreds of lights from fireflies.

The twinkling was never-ending and as I looked around at other fields, the lights continued as far as I could see. The dark green of the soybeans on this July evening gave the very best background, better than the oat field across the road, already changing color from green to gold.

Explaining it to a city dweller, unable to see a tiny thing like a firefly, I can only compare it to flying into Los Angeles and seeing the myriad of lights in the foothills before the continuous bright lights of the city.

The twinkling is a prelude to the heavenly stars that will be visible in another hour. Our farmyard has no yard light and has always been a great spot for looking at the Milky Way, the North Star or the Big Dipper. When my younger son was attending college in Ohio, he brought one of his friends home for a visit. The friend grew up in Cleveland, Ohio, surrounded by city lights. He had never seen the Milky Way! My son was amazed, and pleased, that he was able to introduce Will to the nighttime sky.

Soybean Field in Daylight

Detour

Our daughter was married last week in Orange County, California. I was scheduled to sing "The Lord's Prayer" during the ceremony.

On the morning of the wedding I felt it more important than ever to get out early for some exercise. I walked to the end of her street north and back south. But it was taking forever!

All the townhouses looked the same. Finally, I looked at the house numbers and realized an extra block or two south does take time. I know I'd never make the same mistake walking down a road in the country, where there are no more than one or two houses in a mile and they certainly never look the same.

Her wedding was in the Crystal Cathedral and the pastor was from northwest Iowa. It was comforting to meet someone in California who knew about country roads and farming in our part of the nation. Jeanna, one of my cousins, sang two songs during the ceremony and was prepared to sing mine. Despite the organist and the church's wedding consultant telling my daughter the mother of the bride would be too emotionally involved to be able to sing, I did!

One of the best compliments I ever received was hearing that Uncle Jay said, "Oh, my God!" near the end of the song. Uncle Jay, an avid opera and symphony attendee, was special for more reasons than just this. He was trained as a doctor but was a farmer at heart and would have appreciated what I've learned while walking a country road.

Singing "The Lord's Prayer" in the Crystal Catherdral 8-1-1998

Birds on Attack

Most of them are plain old blackbirds. They have a high-pitched screech and a peculiar scolding sound as they flit across the road above my head. Some merely sit on the electrical lines on the south side of the road, scolding as I walk by.

I didn't begin my morning walks until late May. Perhaps the first batch of babies were well on their way at that time. Now, there must be a second brood in the nest. Things have become much more serious.

Last week was the first time I had been dive-bombed in many years. It surprised me. Two blackbirds took turns diving within three feet of my head. My first reaction was to duck. The second reaction was to say, "Please don't do anything else to my head!"

At the corner, I turned north. A quarter mile further north sat a large group – silent, watching. I was not worth wasting even a few comments. All flew away but one, and then she gave me quite a tongue-lashing.

Last evening a solitary mourning dove sat serenely on a wire while I passed to the west and back to the east. There was no aerial attack, no scolding. Perhaps she had decided that I was so insignificant she need not be bothered.

Bird on a Wire

Cobblestones

Like old-world cobblestones, meticulously cut and laid by skilled artisans, my country road is hard as concrete. Not the whole mile, you understand, but just the 500 feet directly in front of the house.

Our roads in Pocahontas County, Iowa, are made of limestone. The rock is plentiful in the southeastern part of the county and it makes a very solid pathway on nearly every square mile of the county.

The solidity is offset by the dust that is constantly rubbed off the rock as traffic drives over it. Sometimes a limestone cloud can be like dense fog as it rolls past the house. It has been worse the last few years as more truck traffic speeds past the house.

For the past twenty or more years the county has sprayed a chemical on the road past the house (at a hefty price, of course). It reduces the dust for a few weeks – not nearly long enough for a lasting effect. Only after the second application of chemicals in August will the limestone change into the cobblestone appearance. Soon, snow and ice will keep the dust at bay for a few months. Of course, winter makes new challenges on our country road.

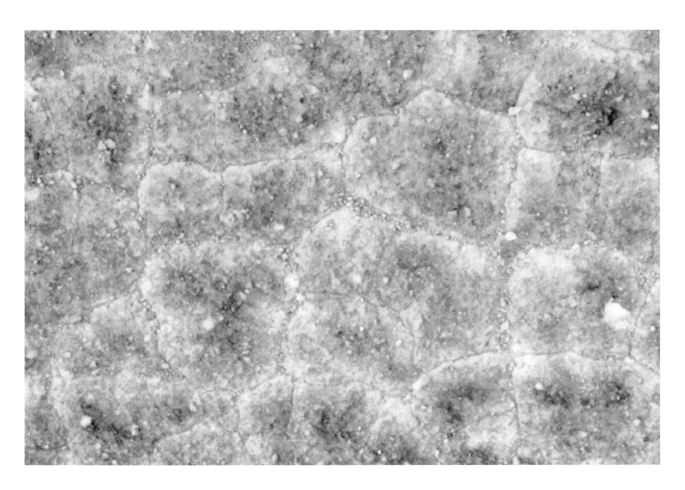

Unpaved Limestone Road

Good Dog

We inherited a dog that was not welcome in a city apartment. She was a small Pekingese who thought she was a Saint Bernard. Barking at cars on the road or in the yard was her favorite job.

When I went for a walk the first time after her arrival, it didn't occur to me she would follow. I walked a quarter mile west, a quarter mile north. As I turned back south, I could see a small white dog crossing the intersection! We had a problem.

Considerable shouting and running toward her was enough to scare her home. But how to train her to stay in the yard while I walked out of sight? I eventually learned that she had been taught to "stay" and after a few refresher lessons, she sat in our driveway while I walked either direction.

Every spring the lessons had to be retaught. "Stay!" she is told as I walk a hundred yards to the east. "Good Dog!" if she stayed in the driveway. "Stay!", as I walk to the west. "Good Dog!"

When she was good, she was praised to the heavens, told we could "sit" and she bounded ahead of me to the front steps. We sat, I petted and told her how great she was. She smiled, as only a Pekingese can smile and her curly tail wagged. She knew she was a good dog!

Sassy – Pekingese with a Summer Haircut

The Ol-factor

When walking a country road, you will sometimes find wild roses in the gravel at the edge. I once tried to dig one by jumping on the spade with both feet, only to have the hard ground kick me back. I found myself sitting on the ground looking at the lovely rose. It stayed where it was planted, still as fragrant as ever.

Other fragrances from my memory are still there along a country road. How about mown alfalfa, the juice of asparagus as you break it off after finding it in the fencerow, lilacs in the neighbor's yard? There is nothing quite as sweet…unless it is the smell of freshly-cut Kentucky Bluegrass.

Somewhere, deep in my brain, is the memory of the fragrance of recently turned, dark, moist soil. Fifty years ago, every farmer used the mold-board plow to turn the soil over to a depth of 6 to 8 inches.

We considered it a thing of beauty. For too many years, the prairie winds stole our topsoil before the Midwest humans decided to preserve it. Some of us still remember the dust storms as late as the 1970's and are thankful they are history.

Today a few farmers are still making their fields black in spring. But, for the majority, the beautiful field at planting time is the one with trash (soybean stubble or crushed corn stalks) still laying on the surface. Last spring an Ohio friend sent a photo of his first pass plowing a field. The field was green and when I asked if he plants the now-recommended winter cover crop, he replied, "No…too much rain this spring…just weeds." Whatever saves the soil!

Black Soil - Conserved Soil

Peaceable Kingdom

How I wish I'd had a camera with me that warm summer evening! The twenty or so cows with their calves made a habit of coming to one corner. It was the highest point in the pasture where they could enjoy the evening breeze and escape the flies and mosquitoes. It has always been a peaceful time of day and a calming scene when we drive past to check on the calf crop.

That summer, others shared the pasture. We had a group of miniature horses, a quarter horse and a donkey. They appreciated the breezes, also. We all just stood, looking at each other. The equines had been taught to obey when I told them to back up, for my safety, so each could be petted individually. Occasionally, a curious calf would come closer to me as I talked to and petted each of the equines. A few wise old cows moved toward me, curious but unafraid.

The scripture about how the lion and the lamb would someday lie down together came to mind. There were no dangerous animals in the pasture. Even the bull was a quiet kind of guy. I spent nearly a half-hour in that peaceful corner of my world, marveling at the creatures God has created. I carried that feeling of peace all the way back to the house and it comes back each time I remember those special animals.

Cattle on Pasture

Canadian Geese

There's a creek at the north edge of our farm, down a half-mile of country road from the house. It starts in Minnesota and winds its way through two Iowa counties before reaching us. A pasture surrounds the creek, usually occupied by a herd of 20 beef cows and their calves during the summer months.

Other occupants of the pasture and creek are several pairs of Canadian geese, raising their babies on the grass and, later, the corn which surrounds the pasture. With the pasture a half-mile from the house, I seldom hear any honking by the parents as they herd their flock. But walking on the bridge that crosses the creek just might cause a ruckus as the brood is gathered.

By September the corn field turns brown and occasional ears drop to the ground. Careful search can become breakfast, lunch and dinner for the brood. After the combine takes most of the corn, ears left on the ground make meals so much easier.

Although there is some discussion taking place while the group is on the ground, during the day the honking becomes much louder as they fly to various fields in the neighborhood. There is no other sound so connected with autumn as the sound of a flock of geese flying overhead.

Goose on the Lawn

Autumn Colors

The crisp evening air this October made me walk a bit faster, swinging my arms to create a warming effect. A group of birds – sparrows, maybe – flew off the road ahead of me. Some grain spilled from a farm wagon yesterday would help feed sparrows and pheasants for the next few days.

This kind of day is one to treasure. I walked west as the sun was still a bit high in the sky and would not be setting for another hour or more. Clouds gather on the western horizon, hinting of rain by morning. Most farmers have had dry weather for harvest this year and need a day or two of rain for rest and repairing of machinery.

Turning around at the mile marker, I started walking back toward the house. What I had missed going west was now brightly visible. The Japanese Maple shrubs on the west side of the grove were the most brilliant in several years. The lack of rain the past month had given the trees a chance to pour out gold and orange colors to challenge any box of crayons. Neighbors often mention how much they enjoy our trees as they drive past. Thank You, Lord, for your gift of nature!!

West Side of the Grove

Aging in Place in 2020

We still live on that country road, though I no longer walk on it. The increase in hog confinement buildings in our county has resulted in an increased number of large feed trucks traveling on our road…often at great speed. Some neighbors drive cars and pickups at fast speeds. It is no longer safe.

It seems there are a lot of things we can no longer do outside. The road dust is a constant occurrence during the warm months. I go out early in the morning when traffic is minimal to water new plants and enjoy the sound of birds waking the world.

Thinking of years ahead and the need to move to a smaller place, with fewer trees and animals, sometimes makes me sad. But the thought of having neighbors across the street to visit, sidewalks for safe walking, someone else responsible to clean snow off the driveway…some of these things make me look forward to the future.

Most of all I am thankful that I can still walk, am aging in this safe place in Iowa, and can look forward to a future with new adventures at age eighty.

Printed in the United States
By Bookmasters